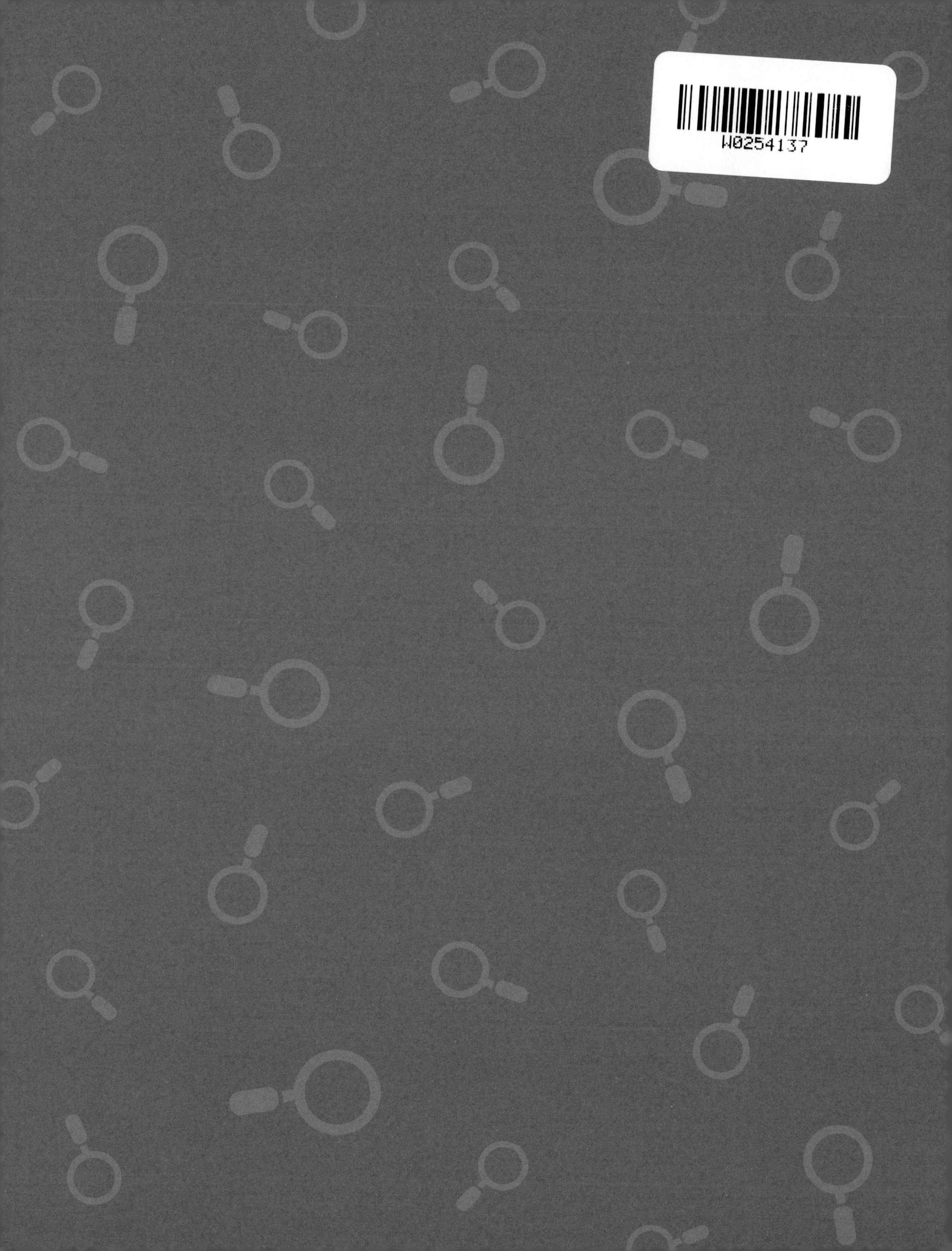
W0254137

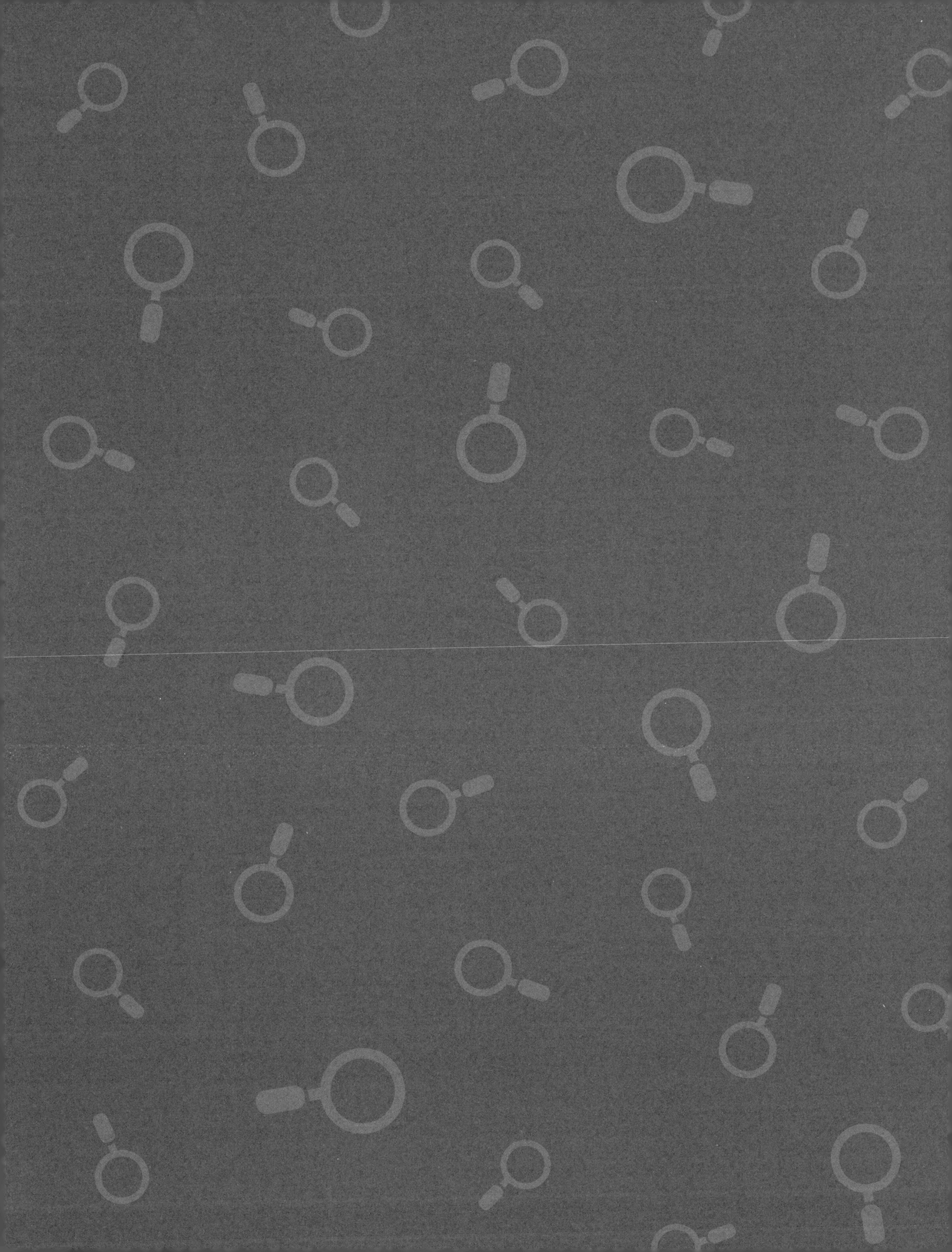

ANCIENT GREEKS

GET HANDS-ON WITH HISTORY

Written by Jane Lacey

W
FRANKLIN WATTS
LONDON • SYDNEY

Franklin Watts
First published in Great Britain in 2021
by The Watts Publishing Group

Produced for Franklin Watts by
White-Thomson Publishing Ltd
www.wtpub.co.uk

HB ISBN: 978 1 4451 7727 4
PB ISBN: 978 1 4451 7743 4

Editor: Katie Dicker
Designer: Clare Nicholas
Series designer: Rocket Design (East Anglia) Ltd

Picture credits:
t=top b=bottom m=middle l=left r=right

Shutterstock: SofiaV *cover/title page l*, AikStudio *cover/title page r*, Unitone Vector 4 and 12b, delcarmat 5tl, 5br, 12t, 17t, 20b, 24t, 24b, 30t, 31t, paseven 5tr, 11t and 31b, Multipedia 6–7b, mart 7t, vkilikov 7b, Gayrat Talibov 8t and 30b, Nikola Knezevic 8t, GOKHALE 8m, Massimo Todaro 8b, Yashkin Ilya 13t, Pecold 14br, Duda Vasilii 16b, Oceloti 16–17b, rudall30 18tl and 29b, silavsale 18bl, Ververidis Vasilis 19t, A-R-T 20r, Maljalen 21t, Prostock-studio 21b and 27br, Valentina Vectors 22t and 29t, nimograf 22–23b, GoodStudio 24–25b, ANNA_KOVA 24bl and 28, BlueRingMedia 25t, Anastasios71 26t, Everett Collection 26b and 31m, MarySan 26–27b, madjembe 27t, German Vizulis 27b; istock: Mlenny 9t and 32, duncan1890 16t, HultonArchive 18m, Grafissimo 18b, Em Campos 22b; Alamy: North Wind Picture Archives 10t and 10b, funkyfood London - Paul Williams 14t, Chronicle 14bl, Cultural Archive 15t; Ian Thompson 6bl.

All design elements from Shutterstock.
Craft models from a previous series made by Anna-Marie D'Cruz/photos by Steve Shott.

Every attempt has been made to clear copyright. Should there be any inadvertent omission, please apply to the publisher for rectification.

Printed in China

Franklin Watts
An imprint of
Hachette Children's Group
Part of The Watts Publishing Group
Carmelite House
50 Victoria Embankment
London EC4Y 0DZ

An Hachette UK Company
www.hachettechildrens.co.uk

The website addresses (URLs) included in this book were valid at the time of going to press. However, it is possible that contents or addresses may have changed since the publication of this book. No responsibility for any such changes can be accepted by either the author or the publisher.

ANCIENT GREEKS

GET HANDS-ON WITH HISTORY

W
FRANKLIN WATTS
LONDON • SYDNEY

CONTENTS

Words that appear in **bold** can be found in the glossary on pages 28–29.

THE GREEKS

The Ancient Greeks lived on mainland Greece and on the islands in the Mediterranean Sea that surround it. They were ideally positioned between Africa, Asia and Europe.

Ancient Greece

The Ancient Greeks began to build cities as early as 1700 BCE. Their **civilisation** lasted for more than 2,000 years. In 146 BCE, Greece became part of the **Roman Empire**. The Romans took on many Greek ideas.

Climate

The **climate** was hot and dry. Mountains made it difficult to travel on land. People lived along the coast and travelled by sea.

Most cities grew up around ports or wherever there was good farming land.

The Greeks were famous for their **architecture**. They used these three column styles – (left to right) Ionic, Doric and Corinthian.

Trade and travel

The Greeks were great builders and sailors. They became rich and successful through trade with other Mediterranean countries. Grain was imported from the Black Sea, timber from Italy, and gems, **ivory**, **linen** and **papyrus** from Egypt.

Democracy

The Ancient Greeks had a rich **culture** of learning, art and architecture. They had a system of **government** called **democracy** – rule by the people. Today, many countries of the world have governments based on Ancient Greek democracy.

Pericles was a statesman from Athens who developed democracy as a form of government.

CITY STATES

Ancient Greece was broken up into a series of city states. A city state was made up of the city and the countryside that surrounded it.

Athens

The city state of Athens was a centre of culture and learning. It was near the sea and surrounded by **fertile** valleys. Silver, lead and marble from the nearby hills and a strong **navy** helped to make it rich and powerful. Athenians and Spartans enjoyed wealth partly, too, because much of the work in both city states was done by slaves.

Soldiers in Sparta spent over 20 years training for battle.

Sparta

The city state of Sparta was warlike. All young men trained as soldiers and the Spartan army was known for its toughness and bravery. Sparta had two kings which was unusual. If one king was at war, the other could rule.

Athens and Sparta fought against each other in the Peloponnesian War (431–404 BCE). This war divided Ancient Greece and made it weak.

Parthenon

A temple called the Parthenon was built to celebrate the glory of Athens in 438 BCE. Classical Greek architecture like this has been copied all over the world.

The ruins of the Parthenon can be seen on a hill above Athens.

ACTIVITY

MAKE A MODEL OF THE PARTHENON

You will need:

- **A4 white card**
- **A4 blue card**
- **pencil**
- **scissors**
- **felt-tip pens**
- **glue**

1. Draw the front view of the Parthenon on white card, adding tabs at the top. Allow an extra panel along the bottom to fold back. Cut out carefully.

2. Add on the details in a light-coloured felt-tip: the grooves on the pillars, and the decorations on the roof.

3. Fold a strip of card like a fan for the steps and glue.

4. Fold back the tabs and stick them onto A4 blue card to give a 3D effect.

DAILY LIFE

Greek houses were made of mud bricks and plaster with clay tiles on the roofs. Rooms were arranged around a courtyard with a well in the centre. Windows were small with wooden shutters to keep out the warm sunlight.

Wealthier homes were made from stone or marble.

Men and women

Men were **citizens** with the right to vote and work. Women could not vote and had to obey their husbands. They looked after the home and spent their time caring for the children, cooking, **spinning** and weaving.

In rich families, women ate in a different room to men.

Food and drink

People ate porridge, bread, figs, grapes and olives, which all grew locally. Goats provided milk and cheese, and hens provided eggs. In poorer homes, meat was only eaten on feast days, but there was plenty of fish. Wealthier Greeks hunted deer and **boar**. Red clay pots were made to store food and drink.

Amphorae were storage jars for wine, oil or olives. They had two handles.

ACTIVITY

MAKE GREEK AMPHORAE

You will need:

- **orange and black card**
- **pencil**
- **scissors**
- **glue**

1. Copy this shape onto card: two copies onto orange card, another onto black card. Make it as big as this page. Cut out.

2. Copy a simple shape onto the middle of the black card vase shape.

3. Cut out carefully as if it were a stencil. Make one cut through from the base to make cutting out simpler.

4. Stick the cut-out shape onto one orange pot and the outline onto the other orange pot, to make two Greek amphorae.

CHILDHOOD

In Ancient Greece, boys and girls were brought up differently. Girls stayed at home while boys went to school. Boys grew up to be citizens and soldiers and only sons could inherit the family wealth.

To mark the end of childhood, boys gave their toys to the god Apollo, and girls to the goddess Artemis.

Growing up

When children were 12 or 13, they gave up their toys to show that their childhood was over. Boys from poorer families helped to farm the land. Mothers taught their girls how to run the house, with skills such as cooking, cleaning and weaving.

Children dressed like their parents and followed their example.

Toys and games

Greek children played with wooden carts, spinning tops, hoops, yo-yos and dolls. They played games of chase and blind-man's bluff and a game rather like cricket. They also played knucklebones, a game a bit like modern jacks.

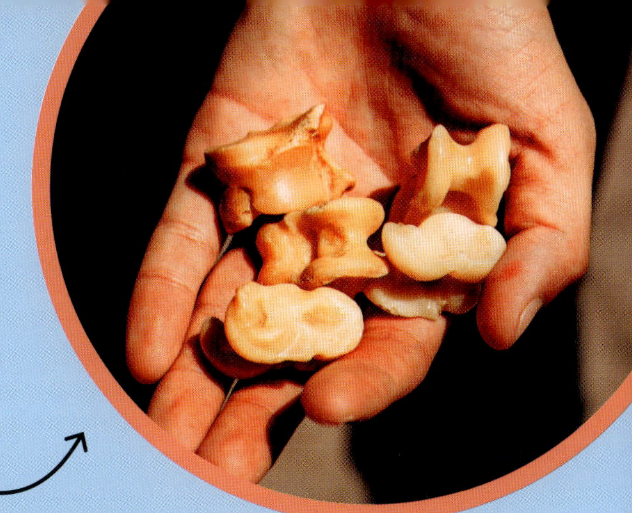

The bones of small animals were used for a game of 'knucklebones'.

ACTIVITY

MAKE AND PLAY KNUCKLEBONES

You will need:

- **newspaper**
- **bowl of water**
- **PVA glue**
- **yellow paint**

1. Tear up newspaper and put the pieces into a bowl of water and PVA glue.

2. Squeeze the water out to make small lumps of papier mâché. Curl your fingers around each lump to make a knucklebone shape. You'll need about eight bones.

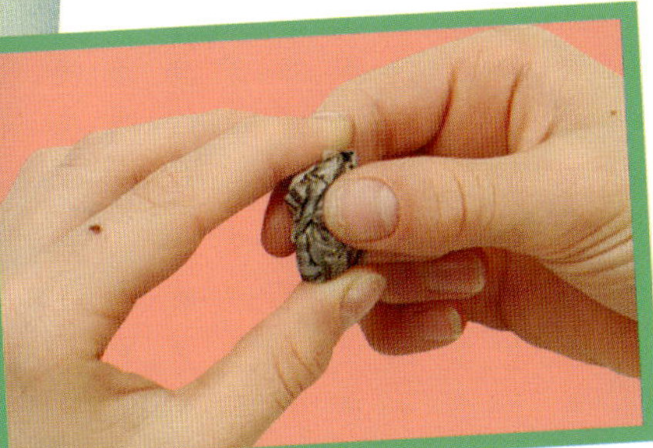

3. Let the knucklebones dry thoroughly.

4. Paint yellow and varnish with a layer of watered-down PVA glue.

HOW TO PLAY KNUCKLEBONES

Game A (6 bones)

Spread the fingers of one hand on the ground. Throw one bone in the air with the other hand. Try and knock another bone into a space between your fingers before you catch it. Try and get all five bones in place.

Game B

Throw the bones in the air and catch as many as you can on the back of your hand.

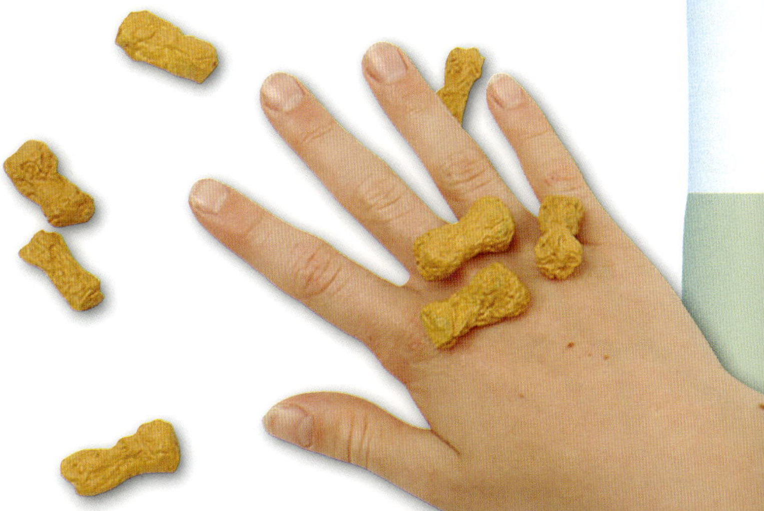

CLOTHES

The Ancient Greeks wore light, loose clothes, leather sandals and hats to protect them from the hot Sun. Clothes were made of fine wool or linen. The rich wore silk from China.

This ancient Greek jar was used to store perfume. Women also wore make-up.

Daily wear

Men and women wore a chiton, which was a **tunic** fastened with brooches at the shoulders and a belt around the waist. A cloak or shawl called a himation was an additional covering. Children wore short tunics. Some Greeks walked barefoot but most wore leather sandals. Women spent lots of time on their appearance and had elaborate hairstyles.

Clothes were made from cotton and linen (or wool in winter).

chiton

himation

Headbands were made from leaves or metal, like this gold leaf band.

Jewellery

Rich families wore gold and silver jewellery to show their wealth and status. The less wealthy had jewellery of bronze, lead, iron and glass. People were often buried with their most precious jewellery.

These gold earrings from Ancient Greece are thought to date from 300 BCE.

ACTIVITY

MAKE GOLD EARRINGS

You will need:

- **gold string**
- **gold card**
- **pencil**
- **ruler**
- **scissors**
- **8 beads**

1. Cut eight 5 cm lengths and two 10 cm lengths of gold string (for loops).

2. Copy the shapes below onto gold card and cut them out. Score on patterns with a blunt pencil.

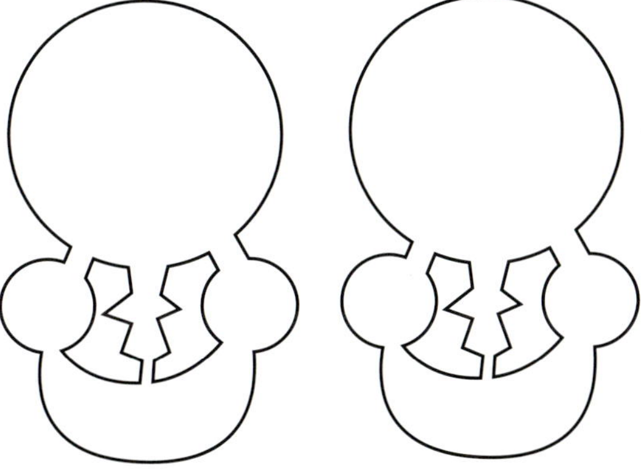

3. Make a hole at the top of the large circle shapes and four holes along the bottom of each earring.

4. Thread gold string through each of the holes along the bottom and tie. Attach a bead and knot.

5. Attach a loop at the top to hang around your ears.

RELIGION AND MYTHS

The Greeks worshipped many gods and goddesses. Public festivals were held to make the gods happy so they would grant the people's wishes and protect them from danger. A festival could be a play, an athletic competition or a procession.

Temples

Temples were the most magnificent buildings in the city. A temple was a god's home on Earth. People brought animals or birds to the temple, where a priest **sacrificed** them to the gods. At home, people had a small **altar** where the family worshipped every day.

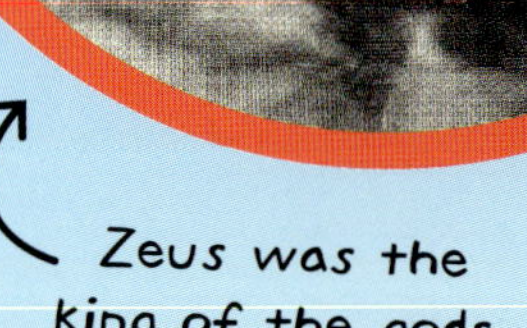

Zeus was the king of the gods.

The most elaborate temples were made from marble.

The myth of Icarus

Myths are stories about gods, goddesses and heroes that teach important life lessons. Icarus's father Daedalus made his son wings of wax and feathers. He warned Icarus not to fly too near the Sun. But Icarus disobeyed, the wax melted, and he fell to his death.

What do you think was the lesson of the Icarus myth?

ACTIVITY

MAKE A COLLAGE OF ICARUS

You will need:

- **black paper**
- **pencil**
- **feathers, material, coloured paper**
- **glue**

1. Draw Icarus with his wings and the Sun in the background.
2. Glue on feathers, pieces of material and coloured paper to finish the picture.

OLYMPIC GAMES

The Greeks believed that the gods lived on Mount Olympus and that Zeus was their ruler. Games were held at Olympia every four years in honour of Zeus. The games were so important that all wars were stopped while they took place.

Marathon race

In 490 BCE, the Greeks defeated Persian invaders at the battle of Marathon. A messenger ran 41 kilometres (26 miles) from Marathon to Athens to deliver the good news. The marathon long-distance race became part of the modern Olympic Games when they were started in 1896.

The messenger Pheidippides collapsed and died after running a 26-mile 'marathon'.

PALAISTRA - WRESTLING AND JUMPING

GYMNASIUM - TRAINING AND THROWING

STADIUM - TRACK EVENTS

Over the years there were more events added, each needing a different building.

The first Olympic Games were held in 776 BCE.

Nighttime race

Relay races were held at night. Runners passed torches instead of a baton. The winner lit a fire on an altar to the gods.

Today, an Olympic torch is used to start the modern Olympic Games.

ACTIVITY

MAKE AN OLYMPIC TORCH

You will need:

- **gold and silver card**
- **pencil**
- **scissors**
- **coloured tissue paper (red, orange, yellow, white and grey)**
- **glue or stapler**

1. Copy the shapes below. Make a cone of gold card. Glue the silver card around the top of the cone.

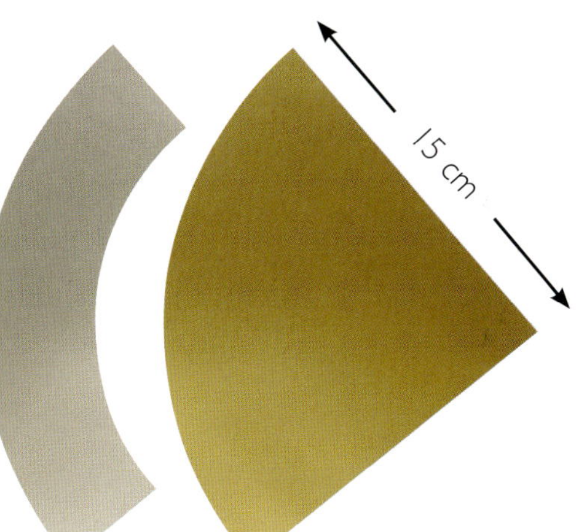

2. Cut flames of red, orange and yellow tissue paper; use white and grey for smoke. Fix them inside your torch.

3. Run, streaming the smoke and flames behind you.

WRITING

The word 'alphabet' comes from the first two letters of the Greek alphabet – alpha and beta. The Ancient Greeks were the first to write vowels – AEIOU.

Homer

The Greek poet Homer is famous for his poems the Iliad – the story of the siege of Troy – and also the Odyssey – the story of Odysseus' journey home from Troy to the island of Ithaca. Homer knew the poems by heart and never wrote them down. The copies we have of his poems were written down hundreds of years after his death.

The Greek alphabet

α	Α	Alpha a
β	Β	Beta b
γ	Γ	Gamma g
δ	Δ	Delta d
ε	Ε	Epsilon e
ζ	Ζ	Zeta z
η	Η	Eta e
θ	Θ	Theta th
ι	Ι	Iota i
κ	Κ	Kappa k
λ	Λ	Lambda l
μ	Μ	Mu m
ν	Ν	Nu n
ξ	Ξ	Xi x
ο	Ο	Omicron o
π	Π	Pi p
ρ	Ρ	Rho r
σ ς	Σ	Sigma s
τ	Τ	Tau t
υ	Υ	Upsilon u/y
φ	Φ	Phi f
χ	Χ	Chi ch
ψ	Ψ	Psi ps
ω	Ω	Omega o

In Homer's Odyssey, Odysseus has to sail through narrow waters, between the monsters Scylla and Charybdis.

Wax tablets and scrolls

Boys learned to write at school. They scratched letters onto a wax tablet with a pointed stylus. Poems were written on scrolls of papyrus, which was a kind of paper made from reeds.

This replica of a wax tablet shows how it was used.

ACTIVITY

WRITE IN GREEK LETTERS

You will need:

- **paper**
- **pencil**
- **coloured crayons**

1. Write the name Odysseus in Greek letters.
2. Draw a picture of one of his adventures.
3. Look for the story of Odysseus in books or on the Internet. Try *Orchard Greek Myths* by Geraldine McCaughrean (Orchard Books).
4. Now write your own name using the Greek alphabet.

THEATRE

Theatres were built all over the Greek world and many are still there today. A theatre could hold thousands of people. Everyone could see the stage and hear the actors and musicians clearly.

Masks were used so everyone could see what an actor was thinking or feeling.

Plays

Plays were performed in honour of the gods. When a religious festival was held, everyone had days off so they could see the plays. Tragedies were plays about heroes and gods. Comedies were about everyday life.

Actors

The actors were all men. They wore masks so that they could be seen from the back of the theatre. The masks had open mouths that made the actor's voice louder.

Amphitheatres were great stone structures, often built in the side of a hill.

ACTIVITY

MAKE GREEK THEATRE MASKS

You will need:

- **card**
- **pencil**
- **scissors and hole punch**
- **papier mâché (glue and paper mix)**
- **paint**
- **scrap material or tissue paper**
- **string**

1. Copy the outlines of the masks onto card. Make them as big as your face and cut out.

2. Cut out the eyes, mouth and nose flap and punch a hole in the tabs at the side.

3. Build up eyebrows and noses with papier mâché.

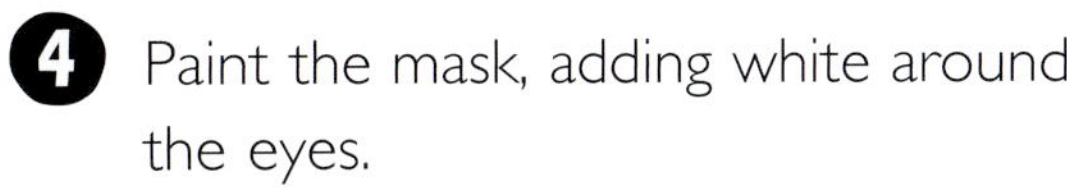

4. Paint the mask, adding white around the eyes.

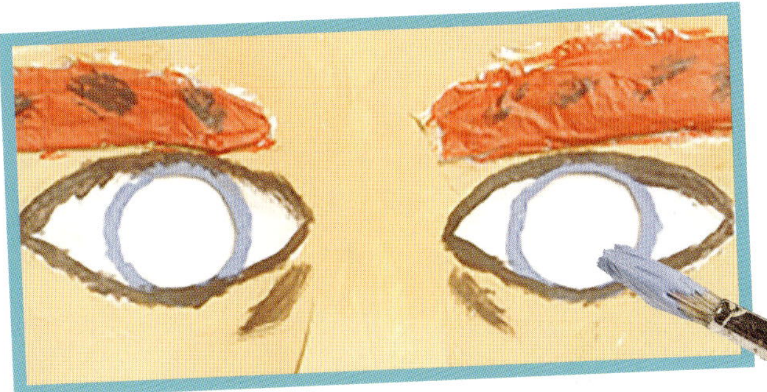

5. All kinds of materials can be added for hair – wool, cotton wool, shaggy cloth, or tissue paper.

6. Tie string through the holes in the tabs and wear.

LEARNING

Traditionally, the Greeks learnt about life and death, and the world around them from their gods, myths and legends. They began to look for practical knowledge through studying history and carrying out experiments.

Great thinkers

Socrates, Aristotle and Plato were philosophers, meaning 'lovers of knowledge'. They explored the way people lived their lives and how states were run. The work of historians, such as Herodotus and Xenophon, helped to learn lessons from the past, while scientists worked to predict and brighten the future.

The scientist Archimedes invented a screw pump to lift river water to irrigate fields. Screw pumps are still used today.

Greek philosophers gave us a new way of looking at the world.

Mathematicians

Greek mathematicians found new methods of calculation, and their work contributed to architectural styles. Numbers were often calculated using a simple abacus made from counters and lines in the sand.

Modern abacuses are made with wood and beads.

ACTIVITY

MAKE AN ABACUS

Ask an adult to help you with this activity

You will need:

- **small cardboard box**
- **ruler**
- **string**
- **16 blue beads, 4 red beads**

1. Use the lid from a small cardboard box. Ask an adult to help you make four holes in each side, about 3 cm apart.

2. Thread string through the holes, lacing on four blue beads and one red bead on each as you go, and tie in place.

3. Make a hole in the top and bottom of the box, as shown, and thread a piece of string from top to bottom.

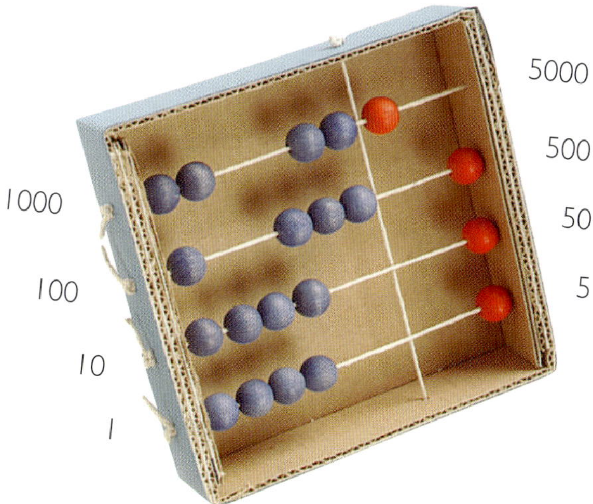

4. The blue beads are worth 1, 10, 100 and 1,000 from bottom to top and the red beads are worth 5, 50, 500 and 5,000.
The beads pushed to the middle show the number being made.
Can you see how this is 7,300?

FAMOUS GREEKS

Many famous Ancient Greeks live on in their achievements, their inventions or their ideas.

Alexander the Great (356–323 BCE)

Alexander the Great was a brilliant general who died when he was only 32. He conquered lands from Greece to India and made the biggest empire in the ancient world.

Aristotle (384–322 BCE)

Aristotle was a great philosopher. He is known for having studied almost every subject possible at the time. He wrote many books on different subjects and was taught by another famous Greek philosopher, Plato.

Alexander the Great (right) was taught by Aristotle (left).

Hippocrates (460–380 BCE)

Hippocrates was a doctor who based his work on the practical study of patients. He discovered that willow bark provides pain relief, which led to the development of aspirin. The Hippocratic oath was a promise doctors made to put the care and good health of their patients first.

Hippocrates is often called the 'father of medicine'.

ACTIVITY

MAKE A 'FAMOUS GREEK' POSTER

You will need:

- **paper**
- **pencil**
- **felt-tip pens**

1. Use books or the Internet to research a famous Ancient Greek.
2. Draw a picture of your Greek (or find an image online). Make it as colourful and eye-catching as possible.
3. Write key points around the image to draw people's attention to their important work!

Sappho (630–570 BCE)

Sappho was a great Greek poet.

Her poems were often sung to music.

She wrote poems about family and friends.

Sappho ran a school for girls. This was unusual at the time.

Glossary

achievement

An achievement is something somebody has worked hard at and done successfully.

altar

An altar is a table on which sacrifices to the gods were made.

amphitheatre

An amphitheatre is a large, open-air theatre used for entertainment.

architecture

Architecture is the design and construction of buildings.

boar

A boar is a wild pig hunted by the Greeks for food.

citizen

A citizen is a free man who could vote and take part in the government of his city state.

civilisation

A civilisation is an organised society, usually based around a city.

climate

Climate is the kind of weather that an area has.

culture

The art, music, thinking and learning of a nation or group of people is called its culture.

democracy

Democracy is a system of government that is voted for and run by the people.

fertile

Fertile is a word that describes soil in which crops grow well.

government

The government is a group of people who make laws and run a country.

ivory

Ivory is a material that comes from elephant tusks, carved to make jewellery, combs and mirrors.

linen

Linen is cloth woven from threads spun from the flax plant.

myth

A myth is a traditional story about gods and heroes.

navy

The navy is a group of ships and the people trained to use them for fighting.

papyrus

Papyrus is paper made from the papyrus reed.

Roman Empire

The Roman Empire was a group of countries ruled by the Roman Emperor.

sacrifice

A sacrifice is an offering to the gods. Gifts of food or animals were brought to the temple to be killed to please the gods.

silk

Silk is a fine cloth spun from threads made by silkworms.

spinning

Twisting wool or linen into long, thin threads is called spinning.

tunic

A tunic is a loose piece of knee-length clothing worn with a belt around the waist.

Quiz

1 Which sea surrounds Greece?

a) Baltic Sea
b) Arabian Sea
c) Mediterranean Sea
d) Adriatic Sea

2 Greek children gave up their toys to which gods?

a) Ares and Atlas
b) Apollo and Artemis
c) Eros and Zelus
d) Hermes and Cronos

3 Who was king of the Greek gods?

a) Poseidon
b) Hades
c) Zeus
d) Atlas

4 How long did Spartan soldiers train for?

a) over 1 year
b) over 5 years
c) over 10 years
d) over 20 years

5 What was Archimedes' invention?

a) A screw to join wood
b) A pump to lift water
c) A bottle opener
d) A type of drain

6 Why did Pheidippides run 26 miles?

a) to get away from the Persians
b) to test himself
c) to deliver a message of good news
d) to deliver a message of bad news

7 How old was Alexander the Great when he died?

a) 22
b) 32
c) 42
d) 52

8 What did Hippocrates discover?

a) that willow bark offers pain relief
b) that willow bark settles the stomach
c) that willow bark soothes the skin
d) that willow bark eases joints

9 **Who taught Aristotle?**

a) Socrates
b) Plato
c) Alexander the Great
d) Democrates

10 **Who wrote the Odyssey?**

a) Homer
b) Hippocrates
c) Heliocles
d) Hercules

ANSWERS 1c, 2b, 3c, 4d, 5b, 6c, 7b, 8a, 9b, 10a

FURTHER INFORMATION

BOOKS

Explore! Ancient Greeks by Jane Bingham, Wayland

The Genius of: The Ancient Greeks by Izzi Howell, Franklin Watts

Invaders and Raiders: The Greeks Are Coming! by Paul Mason, Franklin Watts

Orchard Greek Myths by Geraldine McCaughrean, Orchard Books

WEBSITES

Discover 10 fun facts about Ancient Greece www.natgeokids.com/uk/discover/history/greece/10-facts-about-the-ancient-greeks

Learn more about life in Ancient Greece www.bbc.co.uk/bitesize/topics/zkd9bdm

Find out more about Ancient Greece, its cities and its people https://www.dkfindout.com/uk/history/ancient-greece

Listen to some of the best-known Greek myths and legends www.bbc.co.uk/teach/school-radio/ks2-ancient-greece/zk73nrd

Index

Titles in the DISCOVER AND DO! HISTORY series

- Invasion
- Warriors
- Settlers
- Village life
- Clothes
- Storytellers
- Death and burial
- Kings and kingdoms
- Gods and goddesses
- Religion
- Runes and writing

- The Egyptians
- The River Nile
- Egyptian life
- Clothes
- Hair and make-up
- Writing
- Gods and goddesses
- The Pharaoh
- Temple life
- The pyramids
- The afterlife

- The Greeks
- City states
- Daily life
- Childhood
- Clothes
- Religion and myths
- Olympic games
- Writing
- Theatre
- Learning
- Famous Greeks

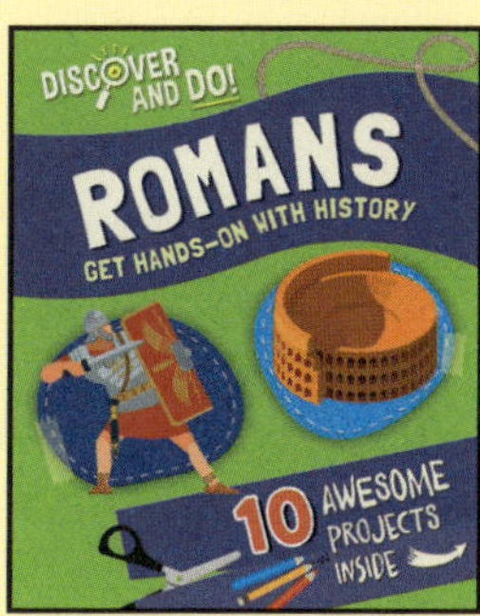

- The Romans
- Roman emperors
- The army
- Life in Roman times
- Houses
- Childhood
- Letters and numbers
- Entertainment
- Roman baths
- Roman towns
- Gods and myths

- The Tudors
- Henry VIII
- Life at court
- Tudor homes
- Tudor London
- Street life
- Elizabeth I
- Exploration
- Tudor childhood
- Food
- Theatre

- The Vikings
- Sea journeys
- Warriors
- Viking raids
- Viking houses
- Daily life
- Viking crafts
- Pastimes
- Life and death
- Gods and legends
- Famous Vikings

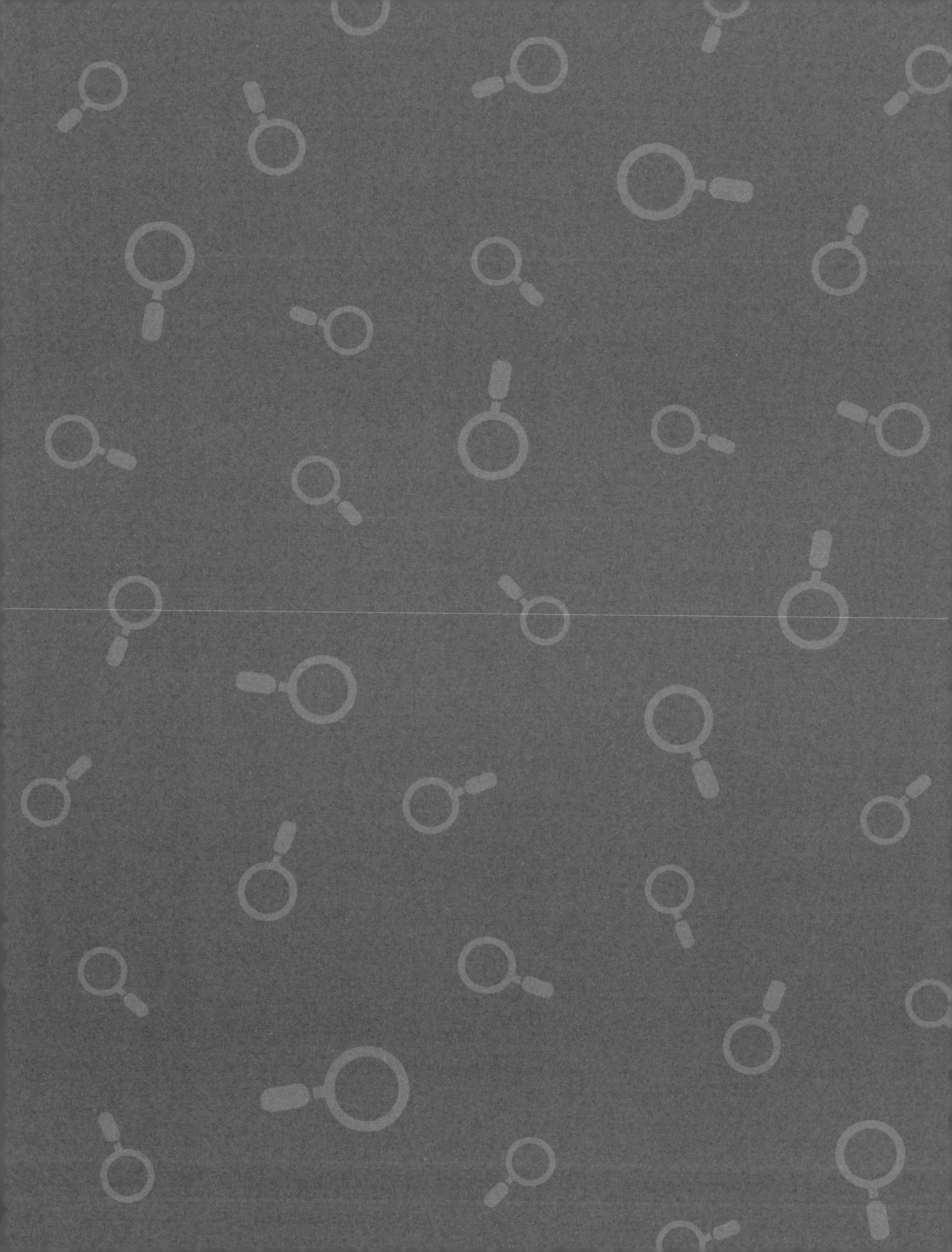